CRAIG AMMERALL, RRT

BreathWish

A Scriptural Guide to Smoking Cessation and Understanding COPD

Outskirts Press, Inc.
Denver, Colorado

CONTENTS

Preface... i

Part I...1

    Chapter 1- A Higher Calling.....................................3

    Chapter 2- Addiction...9

    Chapter 3- Temptation 15

    Chapter 4- Paradise Lost...19

    Chapter 5- You, Too, Shall Conquer!......................25

    Chapter 6- Good, Evil, and the Desert.....................27

    Chapter 7- God's Love... God's Sword 31

Part II 35

    Chapter 1- Back to School......................................37

    Chapter 2- COPD...The Mysterious Acronym.........41

    Chapter 3- Cinderella Story, or Evil Stepmother.........45

    Chapter 4- Beyond the Lungs 49

    Chapter 5- Second is Better Than First?...................53

    Chapter 6- Diagnosing COPD 57

    Chapter 7- Treatment of COPD 63

    Chapter 8- Nicotine and Non-Nicotine Replacement......71

Part III 75

Devotional..79

Glossary of Terms 111

PREFACE

Webster's defines inspiration as *"one that moves the intellect or emotions, or prompts action or invention."* When deciding to write a book, I needed inspiration. As a respiratory therapist, this *inspiration* came from different sources. The first is being the vast majority of the patients I work with not having a true understanding of their disease. The second source came from how we confront the main cause of Chronic Obstructive Pulmonary Disease (COPD)... cigarettes. I just felt that there had to be a better way of helping people quit smoking. Until cigarettes are taken out of the equation, COPD is going to continue to kill at alarming rates. While many other diseases, such as heart disease and cancer, have been pushed to the forefront of medical awareness and treatment, COPD still remains relatively obscure. While many diseases that plague our society are on the decline, COPD's pendulum is swinging in the other direction. I had to ask myself why this is. I have many theories that may or may not be justified, but regardless, COPD remains a societal "black eye".

Working in medicine, it is fashionable to use fancy medical terms to communicate with fellow medical staff.

Unfortunately, many doctors and medical personnel use similar means of communication with their patients. These wide-eyed patients and family members nod in agreement like they understand, trying not to appear uninformed. I believe education is the best way to bridge the gap between patient, family and physician.

The philosophy of education applies to smoking as well. When all is said and done, I think it comes down to choices. Although there are other causes of COPD, without cigarette smoking, COPD would be only a blip on the radar screen instead of the juggernaut it is. A truly informed individual might make wiser choices if the consequences of smoking were better understood.

There was one more thing that inspired me to write this book. Being a child of God leaves one open to another form of inspiration. Webster's defines this form as *"divine influence or guidance exerted directly on the mind and soul of man."* I know that not all who will be reading this are Christian, and that is fine, but the Bible says that as a disciple of the Lord, I am to go out and heal *the entire* world. *"...will place their hands on sick people and they will get well"* (Mark 16:18 NIV).

I could have just written a "bread and butter" book that explains what COPD is and how it is treated. What I felt compelled to do was go deeper. I did want to create an easy to read and understandable guide to COPD, but I also wanted to tackle the root of the problem...cigarettes. Although there are no examples of smokers in the Bible, there are examples of fallible human beings that faced many of the same enticements and traps that lead people to smoke today. Some of them failed—many prevailed. What ties them together is that God used them to show us that we are not alone, and that we, too, can overcome!

PART 1

[The scriptures used in this section are from the NIV (New International Version) unless otherwise stated. Any emphases in the verses listed are my own.]

CHAPTER 1
A HIGHER CALLING

"Therefore, holy brothers, who share in the heavenly call-
ing, fix your thoughts on Jesus, the apostle and high priest
whom we confess" (Heb. 3:1).

My line of work exposes me to people with all sorts of breathing problems. Of these problems, none other is more preventable than chronic obstructive pulmonary disease. Since much of my work revolves around these patients, I am directly linked to smokers. Quite often, part of my job is to get an idea of a person's smoking habits. It is important for me to know how long they have smoked and how many cigarettes in a day they smoke. This information is an important step in diagnosing the extent of the damage incurred on the lungs.

With this interviewing experience, I have heard all sorts of reasoning why people can't, or do not want to quit smoking. In my experience, I have discovered that the people who can't or won't quit fall into three categories. First are those who just don't want to quit...period. These people tend to rationalize smoking by discrediting the information out there, or blaming something or someone else for their lung problems. They don't like to take responsibility for their actions. Therefore, any advice usually falls on deaf ears. Many of these individuals have little or no spiritual life at all, so any attempt at appealing to their spiritual side can be difficult. Typically, these are the most difficult people to reach. If you feel you fall under this category and have read this much of the book—good! I also hope that you will continue to feel inspired to read further.

The second category of smoker I am in contact with is those who know smoking is bad for them, but again, aren't truly interested in quitting. These people usually feel they have done so much damage to their lungs that there really isn't any point in quitting. Others in this group may feel they can't quit despite really giving it a chance. Like the first group, these people are difficult to reach. Many of these individuals claim to have some sort of spiritual life, but tend to justify their habits by not being under the control of a more socially darker vice like drugs or alcoholism. I have a friend who falls into this category and gets very defensive when attempting to appeal to her spiritual side.

The final group possibly saddens me most. These are the people who know smoking is bad, and they know God is displeased by it, yet repeatedly fail at quitting. I was working with a patient just like this recently. I was interviewing her and it came up in discussion that she was a Christian. She told me that during her last attempt at quitting, she vowed to God she would not smoke again. She went on to tell me with a saddened voice, how she'd failed God again and wasn't sure if He would forgive her. I really felt her pain. I could sense her disappointment. At one time, I also had a misguided view of God's character, and empathized with this poor lady. I went on to tell her that the God

I knew would never give up on her and that she should keep trying. I pray for all of these groups of smokers, but those who have a relationship with God add another layer to the dilemma.

All three of these groups present with unique problems when it comes to quitting. Educating them on the disease is paramount, but also getting a feel for their spiritual needs is important as well. Today, most smoking cessation programs usually don't approach this topic. They focus on the addictive properties of smoking, as well as the role habit plays in it. There is plenty of merit to this approach, but the success rates at quitting are still relatively low. Imagine someone who loves God and continually feels like they are failing Him over and over. This sort of counsel can't be neglected, and certainly must be addressed. This, along with a true understanding of temptation, should be integrated as well.

My goal in this section of the book is to approach smoking cessation from a slightly different angle. I want to use scripture as the prescription for quitting. My goal is to have people see themselves as God sees them. I will address those traditional subjects involved with quitting, because integrating them can maximize results. I won't spend much time on habit, because I believe the studies are correct on this. This isn't the difficult part of quitting. Mix up the routine. Keep a log of when and where you smoke. Avoid those times and places—making it difficult to smoke can certainly help. I also believe that substituting good habits for bad habits is beneficial. Chewing on a celery stick or a piece of gum when the urge to smoke strikes is a good tactic. This certainly doesn't mean an individual shouldn't seek other help. My approach is certainly not a gunslinger mentality. If medication helps—by all means use it. I would caution when considering these. I suggest weighing the pros and cons of the stop smoking aids being used, because of the potential side effects. There is also no shame in having a "buddy"—a person to help you stay accountable to your goals. I believe God would want you to seek help with those who have your best intentions in mind. The New Testament church embodied the "buddy" system. The apostles always traveled in groups. Paul traveled with Barnabas, and Peter with James, throughout large portions of their ministries. This wasn't by accident. The apostles knew the importance of having someone to uplift them during times of peril and discouragement. Group cessation programs can provide similar benefits as well.

When it comes to addiction, I do believe God gives us useful insight on this very topic. He knows more than anybody that overcoming addiction can be difficult. I also want to point out the subtle differences between addiction and temptation. These are not the same things. I will relay a story where God truly showed His sovereign grace with one of the great heroes in the Bible. This man dealt with an addiction of his own. He battled addiction until his dying day, and God's presence was still with him.

Temptation in the Bible is seen in many places. Again, I believe that God's word not only has a remedy in overcoming temptation, but I believe that God gives us a blueprint for recognizing temptation. Temptation is part of the spiritual battle that we all face on a daily basis. If we don't know that we are being tempted, then defeating it is virtually impossible. God has the divine prescription to quitting smoking—it wasn't by accident that these pearls of truth were given to us. This was all part of His master plan. We just need to search and have faith that God really wants to help us. Healing comes in many forms. I truly believe God can heal us immediately. We read it over and over in the Bible. I have also seen it personally. I have seen, or know of, people who have been healed from drugs, alcohol and pornography, and yes, even smoking cigarettes. What do all of these people have in common? They let God do the work and give Him all the credit. They couldn't have done it by themselves and they admonish that fact. I also believe God heals over time. I am not sure why God chooses one route over the other, but I know our characters, and the characters of those around us, are shaped by the trials we face and overcome.

When you are finished reading this section of the book, I hope you, the reader, sees God as I see Him. Not a God of rules and regulations. Not a God who is pointing His finger at you, waiting for you to fail again, saying, "Don't fail me again; my love for you grows thin!" I hope you see a God who loves you; a God who no matter how many times we give up on Him, He never gives up on us. Some may be thinking that I am giving a false sense of security. Some call it cheap grace. If people feel they will be continually forgiven, they may sin further without fear of recourse. Nothing is further from the truth. I truly believe that those who understand God's infinite grace have a stronger faith. The desires they once had become a fading vapor. This overwhelming urge to give in to *our* desires is replaced by a peace from above. *"Therefore, since **we have been justified through faith, we have peace with God through our Lord Jesus Christ**, through whom we have gained access by faith into this grace in which we now stand"* (Rom. 5:1-2).

CHAPTER 2
ADDICTION

"Every form of addiction is bad, no matter whether the narcotic be alcohol, morphine or idealism. "
Carl Jung, Swiss psychologist *(1875 - 1961)*

The word addiction amasses many images in people's psyche. It is not difficult to envision a young, pale and sickly-looking girl sitting in a dark, smog-filled alley with a belt around her arm injecting her next high. What about the father who arrived home late after a drinking binge? Worried about his next paycheck, he couldn't help but get a drink to calm his nerves. That one drink led to several. He drives home in a stupor, stewing over his bad luck, blaming his lazy wife and worthless kids. Addictions can be, and often are, like the aforementioned, but addiction can also come in more subtle forms. Picture the man working on the assembly line. Break is in twenty minutes and he is more than aware of that fact. He frequently looks at his watch, as if doing so will make time go by faster. His heart rate is slowly increasing along with his blood pressure. A headache is creeping up on him; sweat is forming on his brow. All he can think of is lighting that cigarette and soothing his stressed nerves. This picture of addiction is less obvious, but likely more common. There is no needle or bottle. In fact, this isn't some deep dark secret that he is trying to hide. This man represents dozens on his job, and millions around the world. He is a cigarette addict.

What exactly is addiction? Some describe it as an uncontrollable *desire*. Others use the term "craving". Both of these words invoke those images described herein. I was able to find a great example of what I believe was addiction in scripture. You see, addiction comes in many forms. We usually associate addiction with something taken externally. Smoking, alcohol and drugs all can be addictive, but there are other kinds of addiction that doesn't come in a pill, bottle or injection form. I would like to stop at this point and tell a story out of the Bible, which most are familiar with, that deals with exactly this type of addiction.

The story of Samson is an amazing one. Samson was an Israelite, more specifically, a Nazarite. A Nazarite was a person who took a vow to be set apart for God's service. God had specifically sent an angel to Samson's parents, Manoah, and his wife. This in itself was a miracle, because Manoah's wife was unable to bare children. This angel of the Lord informed them that this special child, under special circumstances, would do special things for Israel. The destiny of Samson was to begin the deliverance of Israel from the Philistines (Judges 13:5). You see, from the time of Samson until the time of David, the Philistines were a major enemy force in the land and a constant threat to Israel. Samson would be born and mature as a special servant of God.

One day as an adult, Samson was in a town called Timnah when *"one of the Philistine women caught his eye"*

(Judges 14:1). There was no introduction, or "would you like to get a cup of coffee?" There was no courting. Samson would just return home and tell his mother and father, "*A young Philistine woman in Timnah caught my eye. I want to marry her. Get her for me*" (v. 2). Are you getting the theme here? Samson saw a beautiful woman and ignoring the obvious problems with his choice, he wanted her. Not only was he throwing out every courting rule in the book, she was a Philistine. This union between Samson and this woman posed two problems. First, marrying a Philistine was against God's law, because they served other gods. (Exodus 34:15-17; Deuteronomy 7:1-4) Secondly, we can't forget the fact that the Philistines were Israel's greatest enemy. Listen to Samson's comment in this next verse. "*Get her for me, she looks good to me*" (v. 3). Samson never met this woman. Like many do today, like I did many times in my own youth, Samson was fixated on looks. He couldn't get his mind off her. His thoughts were not on a loving, caring, mutual relationship. His thoughts were on her physical attributes. Mathew Henry's Bible Commentary describes Samson's desires like this: "*...but he saw something in her agreeable to his fancy. He that, in the choice of a wife, is only guided by his eye, and governed by his fancy...*" Samson would "get" this woman and fulfill his fancy. This reckless behavior would turn out to be a constant in the life of Samson.

This marriage would eventually dissolve. Samson would find trouble over a riddle he told at a dinner feast. This party was to last for days (seven specifically), and the companions were frustrated because Samson would not reveal the solution to the riddle he posed. His wife cried and persistently nagged Samson every day until he succumbed and revealed the meaning of the riddle. The frustration of Samson's wife's persistence pushed him over the edge. The spirit of the Lord came upon Samson and he proceeded to kill 30 men in the town of Ashkelon (one of five Philistine cities). While Samson was absent, his father-in-law gave over Samson's wife to one of his [Samson's] friends. Samson's violent reaction to this event led to the demise of his wife and father-in-law. (Judges 15:3-6) These events, along with others to follow, would eventually turn Samson into a thorn in the Philistine's paw.

On another day, Samson would visit a prostitute in Gaza. The way in which the author of Judges conveys this account would imply that this was not an uncommon behavior of Samson. Obviously ignoring God's law, Samson would yet again follow his eye, not his heart. Samson would put his life in danger and be forced to escape death by the Philistines yet another time.

Then appeared a woman from the Valley of Sorek named Delilah. The Bible tells us that, *"Some time later, Samson fell in love with a woman..."* (Judges 16:4). This seems more likely Samson's perception of love than love itself. From Samson's previous behavior, we can only surmise that she was another twinkle in his eye. At this point, most know the story. The Philistines used Delilah to find the source of Samson's power in order to defeat him. Of course, we know that Samson's power would lie in his hair. Again, Samson gave in and revealed his secret, which ultimately led to his own demise.

At this point, you may be wondering where in the world I am going with this story. You may be asking how Samson's life ties in to addiction. Like I mentioned earlier, addiction does not only come from external sources. I will tie in the story of Samson with addiction, but first I would like to talk more about how addiction is really a chemical process in the brain.

Science has proven that the two major components of smoking are craving (addiction) for cigarettes and habit. The first puff a person takes from a cigarette results in a chemical process in the brain. There are receptors in the brain. These receptors are stimulated by the nicotine in the cigarettes, increasing those receptors' "need" for more. People who smoke regularly actually increase the number of these receptors, making quitting more and more difficult. When trying to quit, the receptors' need for nicotine takes time to diminish, leading to symptoms of withdrawal. These symptoms include headaches, tremors, irrational behavior, and difficulty sleeping.

I will now reveal what I believe Samson may have been addicted to. Although the scripture doesn't come out and say it, the addiction that I believe Samson struggled with is women, more specifically, sexual addiction. We have seen throughout the story of Samson that he couldn't get enough exposure to women. There are many studies out today that show a link between adultery and sexual addiction.

"Sexually addicted individuals have become addicted to the neuro-chemical changes that take place in the body during sexual behavior, much as a drug addict becomes hooked on the effects of smoking "crack" cocaine or 'shooting' heroin." (*Out of the Shadows: Understanding Sexual Addiction* by Patrick Carnes Ph.D.)

It is estimated that nearly 15 million Americans are sexual addicts. Most of these studies are not intended to condone adultery or sexual addiction, but to show that many of these people need help. The chemical reaction in the sexual addict's brain mimics those found in the brains of people with other types of addiction. Much like the receptors in smoker's brains, those same receptors exist in sex addicts as well, resulting in them wanting more and more.

Samson led a difficult life. Although chosen by God, Samson had many weaknesses to contend with. God used these deficiencies as a means of bringing Samson into deep repentance with Him. Despite disobeying the Lord, committing adultery, and shattering many lives, the Lord loved Samson and never gave up on him. This is evident over and over throughout the story of Samson. The best example of this was at his death. *"Then Samson prayed to the Lord, 'Sovereign LORD, remember me again. O God, please strengthen me just one more time. With one blow let me pay back the Philistines for the loss of my two eyes'"* (Judges 16:28 NLT*)*. God, in response to Samson's prayer, would empower Samson to destroy himself, along with all the people in the temple. Samson was vindicated and God's grace was validated.

"Then his brothers and his father's whole family went down to get him. They brought him back and buried him between Zorah and Eshtaol in the tomb of Manoah, his father. **Samson led Israel for twenty year"** (v. 31).

Those of you who are addicted to cigarettes and have failed over and over, don't be discouraged. Even if you promised God that you would quit and yet failed again— that's okay. Samson failed the Lord many times without the Lord giving up on him. Samson prevailed by true repentance. He learned, albeit almost too late, that there was nothing he could do without the Lord's help. Get back on your knees and pray for God's forgiveness, and pray earnestly for His help.

"Keep on asking, *and you will receive what you ask for.* **Keep on seeking**, *and you will find.* **Keep on knocking**, *and the door will be opened to you.* **For everyone who asks, receives. Everyone who seeks, finds.** *And to everyone who knocks, the door will be opened"* (Matt. 7:7-8).

CHAPTER 3
TEMPTATION

"I generally avoid temptation unless I can't resist it."
Mae West, *U.S. movie actress (1892 - 1980)*

Temptation is a suspiciously odd word. I am not saying it should be taken lightly, but often it is. How often do people say things like, "I am tempted to quit my job" or "I am tempted to scream"? These are more extreme examples, but nearly everyone has heard, "I am tempted to have one more potato chip" or after being offered another slice of pie, respond by saying, "I'm tempted, but no thanks." When people are tempted, or flippantly say the word tempted, I doubt very seriously that the true consequences of that word or action are being considered. You see, this world went from a paradise of sinless existence to a world of hatred, disease and death. Adam and Eve had all of their needs taken care of. They were in constant communion with God. They had the opportunity to partake in this existence forever. What drastically changed the course of humanity was that little word: *temptation*.

When the experts are discussing cigarette smoking, rarely is the word "temptation used". There are many studies that examine the role our body chemistry plays in addiction. There are likely equal studies that investigate how smokers' daily routines feed their addiction. Temptation, on the other hand, is rarely discussed or even considered. It is a concept that is hard to get a grasp of. Words with similar meanings to temptation include: entice, lure or seduce. What do these words have in common? They all imply that a force, or power is leading an individual into an act that is immoral, or against what that individual knows is the right thing to do. As you can imagine, it is hard to do studies or place temptation in a test tube or under a microscope. Science and religion often clash, and temptation goes beyond science into a different realm. When it comes to smoking, temptation is a real thing. It may appear that temptation and addiction are more or less the same thing. On the surface there is some merit to that, but there are differences that truly distinguish the two. An individual does not have to be addicted to something to be tempted to do it.

I will give you an example in my own life where temptation has *nothing* to do with addiction. I know the value of exercise. I know that doing it regularly will have lasting benefits in my life. That being said, I am almost always looking for reasons to not do it. I am actually tempted *not* to exercise. Anything I can think of that can get me out of exercise is a legitimate excuse not to do it. I must overcome my temptation not to exercise on a constant basis. On the flip side of the coin, one cannot be addicted *not* to exercise, as that is impossible. The truth of the matter is that there is plenty of evidence which suggests exercise is addictive if done consistently. Exercise is a good addiction if done in moderation. In my example, temptation trumps, or has a stronger hold over the addictive benefits of exercise.

Like I said earlier, there is a prescription for temptation. It doesn't come in a pill or injection, but through a written prescription of a spiritual nature. Scripture gives us a divine map on how to overcome temptation. Not only does it point out the signs of temptation, but scripture also gives us a remedy. This prescription not only applies to smoking cigarettes, but also has implications in all facets of our lives where temptation can take a grip.

There are two classic examples of temptation in the Bible. One is an example of how temptation is succumbed to. The story of Adam and Eve is the embodiment of how temptation won the battle. This story will help us recognize the mindset of the individual when temptation is yielded to. This will help us understand what we are yielding to is in conflict to what God wants in our lives.

The second example of temptation pits Christ against Satan. What better example than that of our Lord Jesus Christ to show that the temptation can be defeated. This is the remedy. Jesus faced the tempter himself and conquered him. After reading this prescription plan, we will be able to recognize signs of temptation, thus allowing us to overcome it. To make this relevant to people who are in a battle with smoking, I will weave responses I have heard from smokers who are trying to quit or justify their habit. The reader will see some things they may have thought or said themselves. If you are a smoker struggling with your addiction, I hope God will open your eyes.

CHAPTER 4
PARADISE LOST

"So the LORD God banished him from the Garden of Eden to work the ground from which he had been taken" (Gen. 3:23).

God had just finished His handiwork. He created perfection. His human creations, Adam and Eve, were reveling in a world where their every need would be met. They had a constant interaction with God and wanted for nothing. Protection from the disease, and an abundance of wholesome food and clean water, were ever present. God gave only one rule in Eden to be a symbol for the love Adam had for God.

*"The LORD God took the man and put him in the Garden of Eden to work it and take care of it. And the LORD God commanded the man, 'You are free to eat from any tree in the garden; **but you must not eat from the tree of the knowledge of good and evil, for when you eat of it you will surely die'**"* (Gen. 2:15-17).

This would seem like a simple task for anyone. Adam probably thought that eating from that particular tree would never be an issue. This would be the equivalent of being told that if you stick your finger in an electric socket, you will get shocked...so don't do it. Like the command from God, this would be a no brainer. Only one command to obey and Adam would have a constant communion with his creator and an eternal life in paradise. It was shortly after this command that God created Eve from the rib of Adam.

One particular day, Eve would be near the tree in which God had commanded them not to eat. Now follows the first historical account of temptation. This temptation would come from Satan under the guise of one of God's created creatures, a serpent. Satan's attack began by planting doubt in the mind of Eve. Eve responded by reiterating God's command, in particular, the part about death if breaking it: *"or you will die"* (Gen. 3:3). Satan would fire back, *"You will **not** surely die"* (v. 4). By saying this, Satan placed doubt in Eve's mind about God's authority and what His true motives were. *"For God knows that when you eat of it your eyes will be opened, and you will be like God, knowing good and evil"* (v. 5). This "twisting" of the truth was enough to make the fruit from the tree appear overwhelmingly seductive. *"When the woman saw that the fruit of the tree was good for food and pleasing to the eye, and also desirable for gaining wisdom, she took some and ate it"* (v. 6). She proceeded to eat the fruit and gave some to Adam. The rest as they say...is history. Not only would they die physically, but spiritually as well, putting a wall between them and God.

What have we learned about temptation thus far? The following chart should shed some light on the subject.

How We Are Tempted

Eden's Example	Smoker's Example
1. Eve was near the tree.	1. Being near the source of temptation makes avoiding it more difficult. (i.e. cigarettes in plain view, or being around others who smoke.)
2. Eve doubted God. *"Did God really say..."* (Gen. 3:1).	2. We doubt if we can ever quit or refrain from our next smoke. *"I just don't feel like I can ever quit."*
3. Eve reiterated God's command, but still doubted. (v. 3)	3. We read, and people tell us, smoking is bad, but question if that information is really true. *"One more cigarette won't really kill me."*
4. Satan questions God's true motives by calling Him [God] a liar. *"You will not surely die"* (v. 4). This makes Eve doubt more.	4. We know smoking is bad, but question how much it really harms us. We may even second-guess the information out there.
5. Eve gives in. *"When the woman saw that the fruit of the tree was good for food and pleasing to the eye..."* (v. 6).	5. We give in to our doubts, ignoring the truth, and cigarettes become, *"pleasing to the eye"* once again.

We see that Adam would follow Eve and also eat of the fruit. God would respond to their disobedience with harsh consequences, resulting in our world today. (Read Gen. 3:17-19). This account of Adam and Eve also gives insight on how many of us respond when giving in to temptation.

I believe it is important to recognize these responses to help better understand the true consequences of temptation.

Typical Responses When Giving in to Temptation

Adam and Eve's Response	Smoker's Response
1. Adam and Eve avoid responsibility. *"...and they hid from the Lord God among the trees of the garden..."* (Gen. 3:8).	1. We avoid responsibility. *"It isn't that big of deal." "It is not my fault." "I will quit next week."*
2. Adam blames others. *"The woman you put here with me—she gave me some fruit for the tree, and I ate it."* (v. 12).	2. We blame others for our smoking. *"Work is stressful" "Everyone else is smoking; I couldn't resist."*
3. Adam makes excuses. *"I heard you were in the garden, and I was afraid because I was naked"* (v. 10).	3. We make excuses. *"I have been smoking too long to quit. What difference will it make now?"*
4. Adam hid from his responsibility. *"...so I hid."* (v. 10).	4. Sometimes we smoke when no one is around. We hide on the porch or only smoke in our car.

I believe that the story of creation is truly a feast of information. This account lays the groundwork in recognizing not only how we are tempted, but also the results that follow. This is important. If we don't recognize that we are in a state of temptation, then facing and overcoming it is impossible. Like I said earlier, the creation story can apply to everyone, because we all face temptations in our lives. The apostle James verifies our reward when we do overcome.

*Blessed is the man that **endureth** temptation: **for when he is tried, he shall receive the crown of life**.* (James 1:12 KJV)

These are powerful words given under inspiration. God wants to help us—our reward is eternal!

CHAPTER 5
YOU, TOO, SHALL CONQUER!

"It is not the mountain we conquer, but ourselves."
Edmund Hillary

S ir Edmund Hillary likely uttered this quote when asked about the daunting task of climbing Mount Everest. He knew he had the ability to climb that mammoth peak, but had to overcome the doubts in his own mind and quite honestly, the doubts of many others. Defeating temptation may seem as daunting of a task as climbing Mt. Everest. Those of us who have been truly tempted know the power it exudes upon us. I want to use the example of Jesus as to what it takes to overcome temptation. Although Jesus was God, He was also born in the flesh as a human. Therefore, He was to experience the same temptations that we as humans do. The account of Jesus' temptation is taken from the book of Luke. The accounts of Matthew and Mark add insight as well.

*"Then Jesus, **full of the Holy Spirit**, returned from the*

Jordan River. He was led by the Spirit in the wilderness, **where he was tempted by the devil** *for forty days. Jesus ate nothing all that time and became very hungry"* (Luke 4:1, 2 NLT).

There are plenty of morsels to nibble on in these two short verses. I will dissect them in a minute, but it is important to know that prior to Jesus heading to the desert, He had just been baptized by John the Baptist. *"When all the people were being baptized, Jesus was baptized too"* (Luke 3:21).

Jesus was being prepared to go out into the world and begin his ministry. This ministry would include healing, preaching, and casting out demons. He would not have been able to do any of those things without the Holy Spirit. I believe there were two reasons why Jesus had to be tempted by Satan. The first reason, I believe, was because Jesus had to undo what Adam and Eve had done in Eden. It was important for Jesus to be sinless so that he could be a perfect atonement for our sins. He had to be the "Spotless Lamb". *"The next day John saw Jesus coming toward him and said, 'Look, the* **Lamb of God**, *who takes away the sin of the world'"* (John 1:29). I believe the second reason is that He was tempted to experience what we experience and to offer comfort. *"Because he himself* **suffered when he was tempted**, *he is able to help those who are being tempted"* (Heb. 2:18).

CHAPTER 6
GOOD, EVIL, AND THE DESERT

The temptation of Jesus had to be under the most extreme circumstances. Remember, I didn't say Jesus didn't necessarily show us *how* to overcome temptation— He showed us He could, therefore by Him doing so, we, too, *can* overcome temptation. There were three areas of temptation that Jesus faced. They included temptation of a physical, spiritual nature, and an attack on His pride. These are the same areas of temptation we, as humans, face every day. As you will soon see, like everything in Jesus' ministry, He approached this in grand style.

There are two things that I believe are important concerning Jesus' journey. The first significant bit of information involves Jesus fleeing to the desert (NIV). Other translations use the word *wilderness* instead. The verse actually says, "Jesus was led", which implies that the temptation was divinely intended. Both the desert and wilderness symbolize solitude. These are places that can become very lonely, very fast. The wilderness is also the place where the

Israelites failed their test. What should have been an eleven-day journey turned into forty years because of disobedience. The wilderness would be the place where Jesus passed His test. We must also take note of His physical condition at this time. Remember, He had been fasting for forty days. (Luke 4:2) Not one fleck of food had entered his stomach during this stretch. Satan is very aware of the fact that Jesus is very susceptible to the powers he [Satan] brings forth. Satan immediately challenges Jesus to change a rock into a loaf of bread (v. 3). This temptation was an attack on Jesus' physical need for hunger. Jesus immediately repudiated Satan by quoting scripture. *"It is written: 'Man does not live on bread alone'"* (v. 4).

After losing the first battle, Satan did not let up. Satan proceeded to escort Jesus *"to a high place"* (v. 5) where all the kingdoms of the world were in full view. Satan told Jesus the all that lay in front of them could be Jesus'—all Jesus had to do was worship Satan. This was the spiritual attack upon Jesus. If Jesus were to give in to this temptation, that would bypass the original plan of Jesus being sacrificed on the cross. The lure of this temptation would be to elude the suffering that was to occur on the cross. We all should praise God that Jesus did not succumb to this. Jesus responded again with scripture. *"It is written: 'Worship the Lord your God and serve him only'"* (v. 8).

Satan wasn't finished yet. Satan now led Jesus to Jerusalem where they both stood at the highest point of the temple. Satan told Jesus, *"If you are the Son of God, throw yourself down from here..."* (v. 9). Matthew Henry's commentary explains Satan's motive like this: *"By wanting Jesus to jump over an abyss, the devil wants Jesus to presume on his relationship with God, to act as if God were there to serve his Son rather than the reverse. Religious teachers later echo Satan's theology: if Jesus is God's Son, let God rescue him from the cross"* (Matt. 27:40-43). Jesus' pride was at stake here. In essence, Jesus could have said, "You doubt my Father; I'll show you!"

There was a kid who lived down the street from me in my youth. His father was about five foot, three inches and weighed about 120 lbs. We were at the age when a boy's status was based on his athletic ability, more precisely, his strength. This kid insisted his dad could bench press 400 lbs. Genetics and physics said this was unlikely, but who knew for sure. All I know is that kid would walk on hot coals to defend his father's honor. He was a proud kid who thought his dad could do anything. Jesus *knew* His father could do anything, yet did not want to put His own will before that of His Fathers'. Therein lies the lesson in this temptation. Not my will, but thy will. Jesus responded the only way He could have. Jesus answered, *"It says: 'Do not put the Lord your God to the test'"* (v. 12). Jesus' mission was to conquer temptation without using supernatural powers. He was only to use the power of the Holy Spirit who, by the way, is available to all of us. Jesus succeeded at this...so can we!

CHAPTER 7
GOD'S LOVE... GOD'S SWORD

"For the word of God is living and active. Sharper than any double-edged sword, it penetrates even to dividing soul and spirit, joints and marrow; it judges the thoughts and attitudes of the heart" (Heb. 4:12).

Are our temptations any different than that which Jesus endured? Jesus endured physical temptation by Satan's challenge to turn a stone into a loaf of bread. Doesn't a smoker have to overcome physical needs when trying to quit? The anticipation of a smoke makes the cigarette that much more appealing. What about the spiritual attack on smokers? We know it is not God's will for us to knowingly destroy our body. We feel we disappoint God every time we give in to cigarettes. Each promise to God that we will quit only leads to further disappointment when we fail. Will God forgive me this time? Where does pride fit into all of this? We are all creatures who have a certain amount of self worth. When we fail at quitting, we fail ourselves. We tell others about our accomplishments, only to fail again. This beating ourselves down makes it more difficult to quit in the future. We only can fail ourselves and God so much. At some point, we give in to that failure. We have seen, and I will show further, that this doesn't have to be the case.

Remember earlier I said Jesus didn't necessarily show us how to defeat temptation? I truly believe that Jesus defeating temptation, therefore sin, was His primary goal. I also believe that Jesus left us a clear prescription on *how* to defeat temptation as well. Adam and Eve's story showed us how to recognize temptation; Jesus' battle with the devil gave us some clues on winning the battle ourselves. Let's go back to when Jesus was baptized. After John baptized Jesus, *"...the Holy Spirit descended on him in bodily form like a dove"* (Luke 3:22). I am not sure where you stand in your spiritual life. What I do know is upon our acceptance of Jesus in our lives, we are assured of the Holy Spirit. This is reiterated over and over throughout scripture. If fact, the Bible says when we accept and receive Christ we are *sealed* by the Holy Spirit. (Eph. 4:30, 1:13-14; 2 Cor. 20-22; John 6:27) This is the essence of the New Covenant. How does one obtain this gift? *"For God so loved the world that he gave his one and only Son, **that whoever believes in him shall not perish but have eternal life"*** (John 3:16). Jesus came to receive his bride (us) and save us from our sins, but also from the guilt and condemnation from what we place on ourselves along with the guilt others place on us. *"For **God did not send his Son into the world to condemn the world, but to save the world through him"*** (v. 17).

Another clue in Jesus' success in the desert lies in his responses to Satan. Each temptation was warded off with scripture. Jesus knew scripture and the truths therein. Each slash with the sword of life (God's word) took the wind out of Satan's sails. This same sword is available to us as well.

Jesus would go on to win this battle (Luke 4:13), but that same verse also tells us that temptation will return again. *"When the devil had finished all this tempting,* ***he left him until an opportune time.*** *"* We cannot let our guard down.

If you are trying to quit smoking and have failed over and over again, don't be discouraged. The Bible is clear. God loves us so much. There is story after story of God showing His unfailing, unwavering love for us. Let me remind you of the type of people God uses in the Bible to show his love for us. David failed miserably over and over, yet got closer to God than most anyone. In Acts, David is referred to as a *"man after God's own heart"* (Acts 13:22). We read in Psalms, David's passionate descriptions of the love God showed him. We've already looked at the life of Samson, a giant of a man chosen by God to do great things. Samson struggled not only with adultery, but he often pushed God aside, only to return with God waiting… arms wide open. In the New Testament there was a prostitute who many believed was Mary Magdalene. She sold her body to make a living. At the time when she was about to get stoned for her indiscretions, Jesus came to her defense. She repented of her sins at his presence and became one of His most faithful disciples. When the other disciples fled in fear of their own persecution after Jesus was arrested, Mary was there for Jesus, expressing her love to a savior who loved her when she thought no one could. This is the God I know. I hope that reading this book has truly opened your eyes and you see Him as He sees you.

PART 2

[The content of this section is for educational purposes only, and is not intended to diagnose or treat a particular ailment. Please consult your physician for your best plan of care.]

CHAPTER 1
BACK TO SCHOOL

Before I get into the main cause of *Chronic Obstructive Pulmonary Disease*, I want to give a brief anatomy lesson. Without this understanding of the lungs, it would be like putting the proverbial "cart before the horse." A basic awareness of how the lungs work will make all that follows in this section of the book much easier to understand. Throughout the remainder of this section, I will make references to certain anatomical functions of the lungs and their role in the topic being discussed. The lungs, like all the organs of the body, can be quite complex. In keeping with the theme of this book, I will only present the basic material needed to understand the remainder of the information. Let's get started.

In medicine, the parts of our bodies are designated to systems. For example, the brain, spine, and nerves constitute the *nervous system*. The lungs fall under the *respiratory system*. Sometimes, the lungs and heart are lumped to together as the *cardiopulmonary system*. The lungs start with the trachea (windpipe), and split into the right and left lungs. The "tubes" that lead to these lungs are called the mainstem bronchial tubes. Once in their individual lungs, the tubes continue to divide into smaller and smaller tubes. If you were to look at a picture of a lung, these tube divisions would appear much like roots of a tree. In fact, these tubes are often called the *bronchial tree.* As the tubes divide and move throughout the lungs, they get smaller and smaller until they end with air sacs called *alveoli.* Alveoli actually look like clumps of grapes (albeit microscopically). These alveoli are where oxygen and carbon dioxide swap places.

The *main* function of the lungs is this exchange of oxygen and carbon dioxide. Most people know that oxygen is essential for our bodies to sustain life. What is less known by most is the function of carbon dioxide (CO2) in the body. This particular gas is a product of our body's existence. What this means is that just breathing and our heart beating makes our bodies produce this gas. The more activity we do, the more carbon dioxide our bodies produce. People who exercise to near exhaustion will produce carbon dioxide faster than their bodies can get rid of it (can't breathe fast enough). A complex chemical reaction occurs, which leads to cramps. In basic terms, when we breathe, normally 12-20 times per minute, we inhale oxygen and exhale carbon dioxide.

The lungs don't *breathe* by themselves. Assisting this complex system of gas exchange is a series of nerves and muscles that surround the lungs and allow the lungs to inflate and deflate. The muscles consist of the diaphragms, which are at the base of each lung. These muscles are domed shaped. When inhaling, these muscles contract and flatten out, drawing air into the lungs. When we exhale, the muscles relax and go back to normal, deflating the lungs. There are also muscles between our ribs that contract and relax during breathing, and assist the diaphragms. All of these muscles are controlled by nerves, which work in unison in reaction to the environment of the person to balance out this complex machine.

The lungs, like almost no other organ in the body, are exposed to the many hazards of the environment. To combat these hazards, they must be equipped with defense mechanisms to protect them. There are many elements in the atmosphere that aren't supposed to be in the lungs. Examples include dust, pollens, pollution, and yes, cigarette smoke. Our lungs' defense actually starts with our nose. Our nose is much like a filter. It traps larger particulates, preventing them from making it to the lungs. This is why having healthy sinuses is important. Many irritants get past the nose and end up in the lungs. Our bronchial tubes respond many ways. The first is by way of minute hairs lining the bronchial tubes, called *cilia*. These microscopic hairs constantly move in a wave like motion upwards, "sweeping" foreign materials to the back of the throat where it is swallowed or coughed out. The second defense is what are called mucus glands. Much like our nose and sinuses produce mucus to drain or flush out irritants, our lungs produce mucus in a similar fashion. This mucus is often "swept" away with the irritants or coughed out. By keeping the lungs "clean", there is much less chance of long-term damage from infection and environmental insult. Finally, we wouldn't be able to cough without cough reflexes. The inside of the lungs do not have any pain stimuli. What they do have is the nerves, that when stimulated, cause the muscles around the lungs to forcefully contract—causing a cough. As you can see, the lungs are really a group of mechanisms that must work in unison to be effective. Any imbalance can lead to serious problems down the road.

Like I said previously, this basic understanding of lung anatomy and function will really help you understand how COPD affects the lungs.

CHAPTER 2
COPD,
THE MYSTERIOUS ACRONYM

I noted in my preface to this book that we in the medical community like to use fancy medical terms. Some of the terms and diseases are so big that we, as health care professionals, convert these big words into acronyms. An acronym is simply taking the first letter of each word to make one "word". Examples include CHF (Congestive Heart Failure), or CABG (Coronary Artery Bypass Graft). This technique is also popular amongst the "texters" of our techno generation (LOL, Lots of Love).

COPD or Chronic Obstructive Pulmonary Disease is actually what I like to refer to as an *umbrella term*. What I mean is that COPD is actually a disease that encompasses or covers multiple diseases. I will focus primarily on two of these diseases since they, unlike the others, are more directly linked to cigarette smoking. The acronym broken down tells a lot about COPD. Chronic means progressing over a long period of time. The inability of the air to flow properly through the bronchial tubes defines obstructive. Pulmonary disease speaks for itself. Pulmonary means the lungs. In essence, CODP is progressive or worsening airflow obstruction in the lungs.

I mentioned earlier that COPD is an umbrella term that actually encompasses more than one disease. Quite often, these diseases can symptomatically overlap. What this means is that many patients can exhibit symptoms of more than one disease. Ironically, when I was in school, in order to remember these diseases that fell under the COPD umbrella, I used an acronym. C-BABE was that acronym. These diseases are **C**ystic Fibrosis, **B**ronchiectasis, **A**sthma, **B**ronchitis, and **E**mphysema. In this book, what I am going to focus on is chronic bronchitis and emphysema. The reason for this is the medical community has really narrowed COPD to these two particular diseases. While these other diseases are important to discuss, emphysema and chronic bronchitis are primarily a result of cigarette smoking. Cigarette smoking is what I am going to discuss in more detail.

So, what exactly does COPD do to the lungs? In our anatomy lesson, we discussed what finely-tuned instruments the lungs are. We also discussed how, in order to function properly, they must be able to clean themselves. Remember the cilia (microscopic hairs) and the cough reflex? COPD interferes with those cleaning processes. When a cigarette is smoked, the chemicals in them cause many problems. The cilia that "sweep" the lungs clean become paralyzed (cease to function). This means the lungs can't clean themselves. Smokers will often say their coughing and congestion is at its worst when they first wake up. This is because the inactivity during sleep means the mucus in the lungs just accumulates until the person awakens. Since the cilia aren't functioning, the natural cleaning ability of the lungs is hindered. When smoking is continued, the airways slowly become destroyed or "remodeled". This re-

BREATHWISH

modeling makes coughing become less effective. Due to the paralyzed cilia and the damaged bronchial tubes, mucus becomes trapped in the lungs. This leads to areas of infection or pneumonia. These frequent infections lead to more "remodeling" or destruction. This leads to worsening gas exchange, which means less oxygen for the body and increasing difficulty in breathing.

As the years of abuse continue, the lungs become more and more damaged. This insult to the lungs leads to inflamed bronchial tubes and increased mucus production. The excessive mucus production is usually indicative of chronic bronchitis. The medical community has defined chronic bronchitis as increased mucus production for at least three months over two consecutive years. Over time, the airways become more and more irritated, resulting in damaged alveoli or air sacs. These alveoli lose their natural elasticity or ability to return to their natural shape. These air sacs are where the exchange of oxygen and carbon dioxide take place. The destruction leads to the lungs not being able to exhale all the way. This leads to trapping of "stale" air in the airways. This "stale" air serves no function, since it isn't involved in gas exchange. The other problem of this trapped air is that the person always feels like the lungs are full. This full feeling makes the person feel short of breath all the time, because they feel like they need to get the air out, but can't. The destruction of the alveoli is indicative of emphysema. Some individuals present with more symptoms of emphysema, while others have chronic bronchitis. Most present with symptoms of both. Continued smoking will eventually lead to death, because the lungs become so damaged they no longer function at a life-sustaining level. Eventually, the lack of oxygen and the increased work of breathing strain the body so much that the heart will eventually stop.

I know many reading this are thinking that I am painting a very grim picture. You are correct. Some of the most successful programs today do just that; they don't sugar coat the truth. I am reminded of "Scared Straight", which is a program where juveniles who are continually in trouble with the law are brought to prisons where an inmate reveals the horrors of incarceration. This style of teaching is very effective, and I believe can really burden an individual to want to quit smoking as well.

CHAPTER 3
CINDERELLA STORY
OR EVIL STEPMOTHER

In sports, it is common to refer to a team who quietly sneaks up the "win" ladder when no one really expects them to as a "Cinderella story". These are those teams who weren't really supposed to be where they are at, but quietly go about their business. When the focus is on the teams that are doing what they are supposed to, the dark horse team keeps on slaying its opponents with very little attention paid to them.

COPD is the disease equivalent of a "Cinderella story". I know, typically in sports, when we refer to a Cinderella Story we think of something positive or good, and COPD is far from that. While much of society's focus remains on health issues like heart disease, cancer, and social diseases like AIDS, COPD just continues slaying people at alarming rates with far less fan fare.

There are different reasons why COPD remains relatively below the radar. Some of these reasons are justified;

some are just theory (some my own). Since the results of smoking and COPD reach beyond the lungs, truly putting a number on the damages sustained is difficult. Many experts believe that the statistics surrounding COPD are deflated due to under-reporting of the disease, or placing cause on other ailments. Other theories place blame on the government and the tobacco manufacturers. There is no denying that tobacco companies are willing to pay out big money in order to protect their interests. Politicians have an equal stake, since big money is needed to support their campaigns and candidacies. It isn't unrealistic to conclude that the government isn't leaning on tobacco companies as hard as it should, or could. One last thought on COPD's relative obscurity. In our society, the smoker has developed somewhat of a negative stigma. This has made smokers somewhat like outcasts. Smoking continues to get banned in the work place and in social settings. This is certainly a step forward in protecting the non-smoker, but banning smoking doesn't cure the smoker—in fact, it may compound the problem. This person *will* find a place to smoke. This negative shadow cast upon smokers may have hurt them as much as the smoke itself. Who wants to help the bad guy when funds could be used to treat the higher profile diseases? I believe that all of these reasons are contributing to COPD and the "Cinderella story".

Now that we know COPD is out there, where does COPD rank among the top killing diseases? As of August 2006, the American Lung Association has COPD as the fourth leading cause of death in the United States. This may seem remarkably high, but what is more astounding is that many still don't know what COPD is. To shed more light on COPD's health impact, more people die each year from cigarette smoking than human immunodeficiency virus (HIV), illegal drug use, alcohol use, motor vehicle injuries, suicides, and murders combined. Despite these statistics, many are unaware of exactly what COPD is. Herein lies the "Cinderella story". Cigarette smoking accounts for 80% to 90% of the COPD deaths. There are other causes of COPD, but these have much less impact than cigarettes. These include environmental exposures to dust, chemicals and other irritants. Childhood infections also play a role, along with secondhand smoke exposure. Radon exposure, although rare, is a potential cause of COPD. Radon is a tasteless, odorless radioactive gas under the ground in certain geographical areas. Many people unwittingly build their houses in these areas, exposing themselves to the destructive gases. There is a hereditary ailment called Alpha-1 Antitrypsin deficiency (AATD). This protein deficiency causes damage to many organs, but damages the lungs, much like emphysema does. Couple these other factors with smoking cigarettes, and COPD risks increase greatly. (1)

Does COPD discriminate? You would think not, but there is some evidence that sex and gender are relevant. Until 2003, more men have fallen victim from the disease than women. On that particular year, 63,000 females died compared to 59,000 males. Another statistic that doesn't bode well for females is that they are 13 times more likely to die from COPD than their non-smoking counterparts, compared to men being 12 times more likely. (1)

COPD doesn't only cost lives; the financial burden on the health care industry bears mentioning as well. In 2004, the cost to the nation for COPD was approximately $37.2 billion. This cost doesn't include health care expenditures and morbidity (death) costs. These rates are all climbing annually. (2)

These are facts that many people are unaware of. There is good news though. As people become educated, they act. I see it in my own practice—the word is getting out there. The Cinderella story is coming to an end!

References
(1) American Lung Association. www.lungusa.org
(2) Centers for Disease Control. www.cdc.gov

CHAPTER 4
BEYOND THE LUNGS

The damage that smoking does to the lungs is undeniable. Unfortunately, cigarettes' destructive grip reaches beyond that of the lungs and affects almost every other system in the body negatively. I was trying to think of some other item that is consumed by society that causes as much destruction as smoking cigarettes or using other forms of tobacco. I am not talking about illegal drugs that can destroy almost instantly; I was thinking of socially acceptable or legal vices. Excessive alcohol consumption is certainly destructive, but many studies show that alcohol in mild use has some benefits. Caffeine studies continue to show more positive benefits—again in moderation. Sugar ingestion in excess can have some bad effects on the body as a whole. The difference between alcohol, caffeine, and sugar compared to smoking is that word, excess. I cannot find any studies that show beneficial effects from smoking just one cigarette. There really is no good reason to start or continue to smoke, yet millions worldwide do.

I don't want to overwhelm the reader with statistical numbers that relate to cigarette smoking and these other diseases, since my focus in this book is primarily COPD. I do feel that the impact from smoking on the body as a whole is usually clouded by the association of smoking only to the lungs. Most people don't realize that smoking cigarettes can lead to other problems as well.

Prior to my understanding of cigarettes and lung disease, I would have said lung cancer is the primary result of smoking. I believe most associate smoking to lung cancer. The fact is, lung Cancer is actually *second* behind COPD as a result of cigarette smoking. That being said, smoking does cause between 80% and 90% of lung cancer deaths with women edging out men. So, what exactly is cancer? Simply stated, cancer refers to a number of diseases characterized by development of abnormal or mutated (altered) cells that divide and multiply uncontrollably. These cells have the ability to invade normal areas of the body, impeding that part of the body's normal function. These abnormalities can be found in just about any area of the body. These cells often develop into tumors, which continue to grow at an alarming rate. For example, in the lungs, a tumor can block off large segments of the lungs, impeding gas exchange. The tumors can also invade the heart, vessels, and lymph nodes, impeding their proper function as well. The most common cancer resulting from cigarettes is lung cancer. Lung cancer isn't an exclusive result of cigarettes, there are other cancers linked to smoking as well. Smoking can lead to oral (mouth), throat, and esophageal cancer, and is also linked to cervical, pancreatic, and kidney cancer as well. These rates of cancers vary among racial and ethnic groups, but seem to be highest among African-American men. (1)

Most would probably never link smoking to heart disease, but truth be told, heart and vascular disease are also on the list of diseases caused by smoking. The damage smoking causes to the lungs actually makes it harder for the heart to pump blood through the lungs. Nicotine, the addictive substance in cigarettes, increases the blood pressure by increasing the resistance through the blood vessels. This resistance in the blood vessels makes the heart work that much harder to pump the blood through them. Cigarette smokers are two to four times more likely to develop heart disease, and twice as likely to have a stroke. Peripheral vascular disease (PVD) involves those tiny vessels in the extremities of the body, primarily the feet and legs. Smokers are much more likely than non-smokers to get peripheral vascular disease (PVD). (1)

This chapter highlights the extensive damage smoking does to the body. What the chapter does is lend credence to the truth about smoking. It also proves that there is no denying that the effects from cigarettes don't discriminate. The lungs are the primary target, but not the *only* target.

References
(1) Centers for Disease Control and Prevention-
www.cdc.gov

CHAPTER 5
SECOND IS BETTER THAN FIRST?

I would suspect that the words stated in the title of this chapter have never been uttered. I am sure in the sports world no coach has spoken these words in a half-time speech. I believe it was Bear Bryant that said, "Winning isn't everything, but it beats anything that comes in second." There is a mindset in smoking though, that second-hand smoke is not as bad as firsthand smoke. In essence, it is better for you than actually smoking. Truth be told, there is absolutely no merit in this statement. I like to cover all bases when it comes to the realities of tobacco use. I haven't pulled any punches, and I certainly am not going to start now. Many believe that smoking cigarettes only affects them, and what they do to their bodies is their own business. This line of logic may work in some instances, but certainly not in the world of cigarettes or other forms of tobacco. Applying this logic would be like saying it is okay for a person to get drunk and get behind the wheel of a car. Who cares if an individual wants to pickle their own liver, it is their life, right? The fact of the matter is if you smoke around others, they might as well be smoking, too. This reminds me of that old joke that says, "Having a no smoking area in a restaurant is about as useful as having a no peeing section in a swimming pool!" In this chapter, I will present the scientific data that backs up these truths. If I cannot appeal to you about quitting for your own sake, maybe I can appeal to you about your loved one's sake.

Secondhand smoke also goes by the term environmental tobacco smoke (ETS). This is combination of the smoke that comes off the end of a cigarette, pipe or cigar, and what is exhaled by the person doing the smoking. Secondhand smoke contains all of the chemicals and poisons that are inhaled by the smoker. These chemicals include formaldehyde, ammonia, carbon monoxide, arsenic, and benzene, to name just a few. (1)

So who is at risk? A more appropriate question would be, "who isn't?". The surgeon general has warned that there is really *no* safe exposure level. Even just short exposures can damage the lining of the blood vessels, make the platelets become stickier, increasing the risks of a heart attack. Children are at an even greater risk. Secondhand smoke is responsible for 430 deaths a year as a result of SIDS (Sudden Infant Death Syndrome) in the United States. Lower respiratory infections and ear infections are directly related to secondhand smoke as well. (2) Cancer can be directly attributed to secondhand smoke as well. The Environmental Protection Agency has declared secondhand smoke a Group A carcinogen. A carcinogen is a substance known to cause cancer. (3)

What about the mother who smokes during pregnancy? Their baby is exposed to secondhand smoke as well. "Wait a minute!" you are probably asking, "how does secondhand smoke affect an unborn child?" Well, it isn't the smoke itself that harms the fetus it is the chemicals in the smoke.

All of those chemicals in cigarettes inhaled by the mother pass the placenta and umbilical cord, then into the baby. Babies born as a result of a smoking mother are often born prematurely, have low birth weight and birth defects, and often have learning disabilities throughout their lives.

Is there good news in all this smoke? Well, yes and no. Yes, because the government is stepping up to the plate to protect the rights of the non-smoker. Since 1999, 70% of the U.S. workforce has gone "smoke free". Those institutions that have done so have reported increased productivity and decreased absenteeism amongst the former smokers verses current smokers. (1) However, like I have mentioned earlier, although banning smoking in the workplace and public areas have helped with secondhand exposure, it doesn't address the needs of the smoker. That is what this book is for—ha!!

References
(1) American Lung Association- www.lungusa.org
(2) American Cancer Society- www.lungusa.org
(3) Center for Disease Control and Prevention (CDC)- www.cdc.gov

CHAPTER 6
DIAGNOSING COPD

Of all the questions I field from patients, "What is COPD, and how do I know if I've got it" has to lead the pack. This is where I believe both the physician and the patient have dropped the ball. The physician has a responsibility to explain to the patient what is involved with his or her health issues, and the patient has a responsibility to ask questions if he or she doesn't understand. I harp on this often that healthcare is a shared responsibility between physician, family and patient.

There are few diseases that can be diagnosed with one test. In most cases, a series of tests are needed to confirm the existence of a particular disease. COPD is similar to many other diseases, because the practitioner doesn't only want to confirm the existence of the disease, but maybe, more importantly, he or she wants to assess the extent of the damage caused by the disease. This is a why disease diagnosis is so important. Treatment plans and recovery can be greatly affected by how accurately the disease and the progression of the disease are determined. COPD may be even more perplexing, because the disease itself is so broad and symptoms vary from person to person, making the process that much more difficult.

With any type of diagnosis, I believe the first place to start begins with the underused art called the history and physical (H&P). I am not saying the practitioners don't know how to perform a good H&P, I am just not sure they always take the time to do so. So much can be learned about a patient based on their history and that of their families. Things like previous illnesses, smoking habits, and exposure to secondhand smoke are keys to aiding the physician in COPD diagnosis. The physician should also consider work conditions, environmental exposures, and social habits as well. The physical exam is also an invaluable tool providing information that will lend credence to the diagnosis. An overall visual inspection can provide important clues. Observing the patient breathe, listening to heart and lung sounds, along with basic vital signs, such as blood pressure, body temperature, and heart and breathing rate, are informative as well. A thorough history and physical will "point' the physician in the direction needed concerning what diagnostic tests to do.

The following are common procedures a doctor may order to confirm the diagnosis of COPD, as well as assess the severity level of the disease.

- **Chest X-Ray**- The chest x-ray is a radiological exam that takes a black and white picture of the lungs. The white on an x-ray represents bones, such as ribs, sternum, and clavicles, as well as soft tissue such as skin, vessels, and the heart. An x-ray can reveal some features indicative of COPD. Many of the changes seen on an x-ray with COPD are chronic or over a long period of time. One of the chronic changes seen with this disease is enlarged lungs. The air trapping we discussed earlier will make the lungs appear longer. The enlarged lungs may also affect the diaphragms. On an x-ray, depending on how expanded the lungs get, the diaphragms will appear flattened. Remember, the flattened diaphragms will not allow the lungs to exhale fully, making the patient's lungs feel full. The x-ray may also show some scarring and other markings confirming previous infections which are common in COPD. An enlarged heart may be seen as well, which represents the difficulty the heart has pumping blood through the lungs. The heart is a muscle—if it has to work to pump blood through the lungs, it is going to enlarge. This isn't good. Some acute or relatively new problems that may show on an x-ray are pneumonia or other lung masses that may indicate fungus infections, or even cancer.

- **CT Scan**- Another radiological exam similar to an x-ray is a CT scan or computerized tomography. If the physician finds something on the x-ray of concern, this test may be ordered. This test gives a much more detailed picture of the lungs. The scan gives a slice by slice view of the lungs, heart, bones, and any abnormalities that may be present. If things like infection or a lung mass are present, the CT scan will better define the location within the lungs. With the air trapping, the scan will show these pockets of air, which are called blebs or bulla. The actual test involves the patient lying on a table within a tube. Typically, the scan just takes a few minutes.

- **ABG**-An ABG, or arterial blood gas, is a very important blood test to help diagnose COPD. This test involves having a small amount of blood drawn from an artery in the wrist or upper arm. This test is significant, because it indicates how well the lungs exchange oxygen and carbon dioxide (waste gas). A good or normal ABG will reflect good blood oxygenation and a balanced ph (acid/base status). An abnormal ABG will often show deficient tissue oxygenation, which is called hypoxemia, and/or an elevated CO_2 level both common in COPD. The elevated CO_2 level is due to the trapped air in the lungs that serves no function. Identifying the presence of this imbalance is important, because this process is indicative of COPD in more severe cases. Another important reason to obtain this test is because many insurance companies and governmental agencies (Medicaid/Medicare) require this test to assess the need for supplemental home oxygen.

- **Other Blood Tests**- I will only briefly mention these due the amount of tests out there. Some blood tests can be done to check the kidneys, if the body is fighting infection, and the function of the heart. Since our organs work in unison, if one isn't functioning properly, the others are often hindered as well.

- **Spirometry**- This is a simplistic procedure to assess the lung function. The test involves having the patient blow into a small handheld device using different blowing techniques. This test will give a basic understanding of how fast a person can get the air out of the lungs, as well as how much air the lungs hold. If the test shows signs of breathing problems, the physician may consider a more advanced test called a pulmonary function test (PFT).

- **PFT**- This test is the true measuring stick in assessing how much damage has been done to the lungs. Like spirometry, the PFT gives some basic lung function numbers, but can give further details that basic spirometry can't. The test works by having the patient provide the technician with important information that will allow the computer to calculate what the predicted (what the patient *should* get) values are. The patient's age, sex, height, and weight are all considered to get those predicted values. The numbers the patient actually gets are compared to the predicted values. This gives a value called *percent predicted.* An example is if the patient is supposed to blow 100 liters/minute (predicted) and only blows 60 liters/minute (actual), the percent predicted is 60%. Severity of the disease is based on those predicted numbers. The normal range is 80-100%; 60-80% is mild disease, and so forth. The test measures how much air the lungs hold along with the speed in which the air is exhaled and inhaled. Another feature of the test is the ability to measure gas diffusion, or how well oxygen passes through the lungs into the bloodstream. The importance of the PFT is multi-fold. Not only can the amount of damage to the lungs be determined, but another important feature of the test is to determine medication response. Part of the test includes giving the patient a bronchodilator (medicine which relaxes the muscles around the airways, i.e. albuterol), which in some patients improves lung function. This test will aid the physician on the medical treatment side of the disease. A PFT is also a great test to do to help trend disease progression.

Repeating the test every six months to one year can really help the physician in treatment alterations, such as medication dosing as well as alternatives to the medications being given. Many patients with COPD may at some point need some type of surgery. An anesthesiologist may request a PFT to decide how the patient will respond to being put to sleep for a surgical procedure. This test is fairly simple and usually takes about an hour.

- **Bronchoscopy**- A bronchoscopy can be both a diagnostic or therapeutic procedure. This test involves inserting a long, thin tube into the lungs via the wind pipe. This tube has a little camera on the end where the doctor can see inside the lungs. The doctor can inspect the lungs, particularly the larger airways, to assess the damage accrued. Diagnostically, if necessary, specimens can be taken that would diagnose the presence of viruses, bacteria, or funguses, as well as the possibility of cancer. A therapeutic bronchoscopy is done to evacuate the secretions out of the lungs. This can really improve the patient's condition. The test is done giving mild sedation and has some minor complications that can occur. It is usually done on an outpatient basis and only takes a few hours, with the actual procedure usually lasting just 10-20 minutes.

There are also other diagnostic procedures, albeit less common, that may be considered based on the physician's prerogative. Examples include sleep studies, nutritional assessment, and exercise testing. The next chapter will discuss treatment options, including medications, rehabilitation, and surgical options.

CHAPTER 7
TREATMENT OF COPD

T reatment of any disease involves evaluating the extent at which the disease is affecting the individual's quality of life. What this means is that once the disease has been diagnosed, it is important to figure out the extent of the damage incurred. In the previous chapter, we discussed the tests used to not only diagnose COPD, but to assess the amount of damage that has been done to the lungs themselves. Much of the treatment used for COPD patients is based on the extent of damage to the lungs. To better help the clinician decide on how to treat the patient, a staging system was devised to get a better idea of how bad the patient's lungs are. You will see the term FEV1 referred to often in this section. FEV1 is a parameter found in a PFT. This represents the volume of air forcefully exhaled in the first second of a forced expiration or blow.

- **Stage 0.** This stage means the person is at risk of developing COPD. Although these patients have normal lung function, they may exhibit mild symptoms of breathlessness, chronic cough, and mild mucus production.

- **Stage I.** This stage is considered mild COPD and is defined by an FEV1 less than, or equal to, 80% of predicted. Many in this stage may or may not exhibit mild symptoms, and may or may not even be aware they have the disease.

- **Stage II.** The FEV1 is in the 50-80% of predicted range and is considered moderate COPD. Typically, patients experience shortness of breath upon exertion, and symptoms have a significant impact on the health-related quality of life. This is the stage in which most people seek medical attention.

- **Stage III.** This is considered severe COPD and is defined by an FEV1 of 30-50% of predicted. These patients have symptoms that profoundly affect their health-related quality of life. These patients will exhibit many symptoms of the disease and usually require medical help.

- **Stage IV.** This stage is defined by an FEV1 of less than 30%. This is very severe COPD and these patients are in frequent need of medical attention. This stage is also when many patients go into respiratory failure where breathing assistance and death are not uncommon.

Once the patient has been staged, the physician can better determine the treatment needed to suit the patient's needs. The main goal is to slow disease progression. The other goal is to improve exercise tolerance, minimize symptoms, to improve the overall daily activities, and finally, to prevent death.

The first treatment, despite which stage the patient has been placed in, is for the physician and patient to identify and avoid the risk factors that led to the disease in the first place. Slowing disease progression becomes very difficult unless the cause of the disease is eliminated.

At this point, I am going to discuss the medications and other treatments used to treat COPD. The stage of the disease will determine what medications, doses, and what other treatments may be beneficial. I will discuss what might be considered in each stage. As each stage progresses, the treatment considerations change as well. There is certainly overlap, and no certainty in what may be prescribed.

- **Stage 0.** Treatment here depends on how much the symptoms are bothering the patient. These patients who are risk would be instructed to avoid symptom triggers and possibly get the flu shot. Continuing to get check-ups is highly recommended as well. Smoking cessation and environmental exposure reduction are essential (all stages).

- **Stage 1.** This is the mild stage of COPD. These patients are encouraged to get flu and pneumonia vaccines, since those illnesses can lead to exacerbations. Exacerbations are sudden spells of extreme shortness of breath that can lead to hospitalizations and even death in extreme cases. Medicinal treatment includes the use of bronchodilators. These medications relax the muscles around the airways, allowing the air to move freely through the tubes. These medications are typically fast acting and usually last four to six hours. Examples include:

Albuterol- This is a common beta 2 agonist that is more commonly known as Proventil, Ventolin, and Pro-Air. Xopenex is another form of beta 2 agonist.

Ipatropium Bromide- This is a bronchodilator that works on different receptors, but essentially does the same thing. Atrovent is the common name for this medication.

*Tidbit- It is not uncommon to see these medications being used in combination. Examples include Duo-Neb, which is an aerosol form, and Combivent in Metered Dose Inhaler (MDI) form.

- **Stage II.** In the moderate stage of COPD, symptoms become more prevalent. The fast-acting bronchodilators are a must, but long-acting bronchodilators are to be considered as well. These will provide sustained bronchodilation in patients who experience more symptoms. Examples include:

Salmeterol and Formeterol- These are common, long-acting beta 2 agonists that only needs to be taken twice a day. These are commonly known as Serevent and Foradyl. There is a new medication called Bravana that falls in this category as well.

Tiotropium Bromide- This is the newest generation of long-acting bronchodilator. This medication is only taken once a day. The common name of this medication is Spiriva. This is dispensed in a dry powder inhaler. Mouth rinsing is indicated here, because dry mouth is a common side-effect.

*Tidbit- These medications are taken every day regardless of how the patient feels. They are not to be used as rescue medications, because they don't take effect fast enough.

- **Stage III.** This is the severe stage of COPD. The medications previously mentioned are standard treatment. In this stage, it isn't uncommon to use inhaled steroids (Glucocorticosteroids). Inhaled steroids work by decreasing the inflammation in the airways. Examples include:

Fluticicasone and Budesonide. These are the more common medications is this category. They are more commonly known as Flovent and Pulmicort. Asthmanex, Asthmacort, and Q-Var are also medications in this category.

*Tidbit- These medications are being combined with long-acting bronchodilators to improve patient compliance. Examples of these combination drugs are Advair, and Symbicort. With inhaled steroids, the patient must rinse their mouths and gargle after taking the medication to keep from getting sores thrush in the mouth and throat.

Congestion is a great concern in this stage as well, so there are medications that help thin the mucus, making it easier to cough out. Examples include:

Acetylcysteine and Guaifenesin. Acetylcysteine is also known as Mucomyst and is given by aerosol, usually in the hospital setting. Guaifenesin can be obtained over-the-counter or by prescription. Mucinex and Robitussin are common brand names of this drug.

There are also some devices a patient can use to help clear the congestion in the lungs. One such device is called a flutter valve. This device works by having the patient blow into a plastic tube. Inside this tube is a valve that "flutters", causing vibration inside the lungs. This vibration causes the secretions to move towards the larger airways, making it easier to cough up the secretions. There are also devices that can be used externally on the chest wall. A vibrocussor is a device that rapidly vibrates over the chest. Typically, this is a handheld device that plugs into a wall. This vibration loosens the mucus, allowing it to be coughed up easier. There is also a vest that can be used and works in a similar manner.

- **Stage IV.** The severity of this stage means the patient is likely doing all the things already discussed in the previous stages plus requiring stronger medications. Patients in this stage are also spending a lot of time in the hospital, requiring special care and possibly life support to overcome an exacerbation. These patients usually require oxygen supplementation part, or all, of the time. In more severe cases, patients in this stage may require a machine called CPAP, or BiPap. Via a mask or nasal pillows, these machines push air into the lungs, helping with oxygenation and CO_2 elimination.

Medications that are common for these patients include oral or intravenous steroids.

Prednisone and Decadron. Prednisone is often given in pill form. The patient is instructed to take a course of medication and decrease the amount each subsequent day, allowing the body to adapt. Decadron is typically given in a more emergent situation

BREATHWISH

and is often given by injection. These steroids have some side effects that include increased blood sugar, weight gain, and increased risk of infections.

Another medication that is used in more extreme cases is called methylxanthines. This very scientific-sounding medication is actually more common than you may think. There is a reason why COPD patients love their coffee in the morning. The reason is that caffeine is a common methylxanthine. These people will often say that their coffee helps them breathe better. Tea and chocolate also contain forms of methylxanthines. This class of medication relaxes muscles, which dilates (opens) the airways. The medication also helps relieve congestion. Side effects include nervousness or jitteriness, racing heart and diuresis (frequent urination).

Theophylline and Aminophylline- These are the two medications commonly used in this category.

Patients in stage IV COPD are frequently on some sort of antibiotic as well. Retained secretions make infections a constant battle. Sometimes in extreme cases of COPD, surgical options, such as lung reduction surgery or removing the air pockets in the lungs, can be considered. People in this stage may also consider pulmonary rehabilitation. The rehab can be beneficial in helping patients maximize their daily activities. Breathing retraining, diet, and exercise are all part of this rehabilitation process.

Like I mentioned before, these treatment plans are not set in stone, and can vary depending on the individual and the physician preference. Making sure that the patient's total condition is considered is paramount. Many patients with COPD have other ailments to contend with, so tailoring the treatment plan is not out of the question.

CHAPTER 8
NICOTINE AND NON-NICOTINE
REPLACEMENT

U nfortunately, the addictive properties of cigarettes are such that in order to quit smoking, people may benefit from nicotine replacement therapy. You recall nicotine is the addictive drug in cigarettes. These replacement drugs work by reducing the negative effects of withdrawal. Some of these products actually use nicotine, and others use drugs that "mimic" the effects of nicotine. In any case, I don't recommend using any of the medications alone. I do recommend using them with an effective smoking cessation program if you and your physician deem it necessary. I will briefly discuss the different types of medications and how they are used.

- **Nicotine Gum**- Just like it sounds. Nicotine gum delivers the drug by chewing gum. This route is faster than the patch, but still does not deliver the drug like smoking. The gum can be obtained over the counter. Typically, the person chews the gum for about 30 minutes to gain the benefits. It usually takes up to fifteen pieces of gum a day to work, but the patient should not take more than thirty pieces. The patient is encouraged to wean the amount each day.

- **Nicotine Lozenges**- These are similar to cough drops. The person takes a lozenge when the urge to smoke hits. The person should not use more than twenty per day. These shouldn't be used more than three months. Common problems associated with the lozenges are soreness or gums, throat irritation, and indigestion.

- **Nicotine Nasal Spray**- This medication is given by prescription only. This form of administration works well because the nicotine gets to the brain very fast, in fact, faster than any other form of replacement. A usual single dose is two sprays, one in each nostril. The maximum recommended dose is five doses per hour or 40 doses total per day.

- **Nicotine Patch**-This is an adhesive patch that is usually placed on the upper arm. They release a constant amount of nicotine into the blood stream. Unlike the instant "hit" of nicotine one gets from smoking, the nicotine from the patch takes up to three hours to get to the brain. They are usually slowly weaned by lowering the doses over time. The individual using the patch is strongly cautioned not to smoke because of the harmful effects of high nicotine doses. They can be distributed over the counter, or by prescription. Side effects include: headache, nausea and vomiting, skin irritation, sleep problems, and a racing heart.

- **Nicotine Inhaler**- This is a device that a person

puffs on when the urge to smoke arises. Nicotine is delivered in the mouth, not the lungs. These inhalers have a cartridge in them that provides a "hit" of nicotine when puffed. This is also a prescribed medication. Side effects include sore mouth and throat, and a cough may also be seen. This medication is provided by prescription only.

- **Non-Nicotine Pill**- This is more commonly known as Zyban. This medication is by prescription only. It is given while the individual is still smoking, typically one week prior to quitting. The treatment is given 7-12 weeks, depending on the individual. Common side effects include dry mouth, insomnia and dizziness.

- **Chantix Tablets**- This is the latest and greatest of non-nicotine replacement therapy. The medication works in two ways. The first is that it cuts into the pleasure of smoking. Secondly, it significantly reduces the withdrawal symptoms. The medication is given over a twelve-week course. A tablet is taken twice each day. The length of the prescription can be doubled in patients who have successfully quit, increasing the likelihood of remaining smoke free. The most common adverse side effects include: nausea, headache, vomiting, gas, insomnia, abnormal dreams, and a change in taste perception.

This wraps up the educational section of the book. The information provided should give you a good foundation in your understanding of COPD. I suggest you visit the references I listed in this book for further information.

References
(1) American Lung Association- www.lungusa.org

PART 3

This section of the book is completely dedicated to your commitment to quitting smoking. I truly believe that I have demonstrated cigarette's involvement in COPD. What we have also learned is that this disease can be treated, but true healing will not occur unless smoking has ceased. In part one of the book, we addressed the spiritual and emotional concerns that many face when trying to quit smoking. We then discovered God will never give up on us; it is up to us to not give up on Him. He, more than anyone, wants us to succeed. Now that we know what smoking does to us, and that God is committed to helping us, you need to make the final decision. You need to ask yourself, "Do I really want to quit?" If the answer is yes, then now is the time to act.

The rest of this book is going to be in a daily devotional format. I have constructed a twenty-eight day devotional packed with powerful messages from scripture to help strengthen and encourage you. If you recall, God's word is a sword that will help you fight temptation, which in turn will help you quit. I will also provide you with some facts about smoking and cigarettes that will further enhance your resolve.

Before your official "quit" day, I suggest you build up to it. Pick a day that has the least amount of stressors surrounding it. If possible, talk to your physician about ways to maximize your efforts. He or she will help you in deciding whether or not smoking cessation medications may be needed. Your physician can also help you decide if a cigarette wean approach or a more aggressive approach is in your best interest. If you and your physician decide weaning is the best approach, this devotional will best serve you when you have smoked your last cigarette. Once you have all of your ducks in a row, you need to set a "quit" date. Prior to this day, I suggest you really prepare. First, tell others about your decision. Make it a spectacle. This will show them how committed you are and also make you more accountable to yourself. Secondly, get rid of things that remind you of smoking, things like ashtrays, matches, and lighters, which can be a constant reminder of smoking. If you smoke in your house, clean it as much as possible. The smell of smoke is also a constant reminder of your habit. Lastly, I would suggest contacting friends and family who may also smoke. Try to get them to join your cause. If they are not interested, tell them the importance of them not smoking around you. This may involve not being around them for a while until you are confident you have truly succeeded. This may seem rash, and maybe even cold, but remember the big picture. If these people truly love you, they will understand your requests. One other suggestion prior to your quitting—studies have shown that smoking affects the absorption of certain vitamins and minerals, most notably the B vitamins and calcium. Plenty of water and a good multi-vitamin may also help maximize your efforts. This suggestion should be discussed with your physician.

When quitting, your first few days are going to be the most trying. These days are when withdrawal symptoms are at their peak. Once the physical addiction to cigarettes starts subsiding, then the emotional and habitual factors must still be contended with. These are the things that tempt you, and they vary from individual to individual. Be aware of these factors on a daily basis. What are those things that trigger you to want to light up? Like we discussed in the first part of the book, identifying those things that tempt you and being aware of them will really benefit your success. These steps should really prepare you for your "quit" day.

WEEK 1

This week will undoubtedly be the toughest. Like I mentioned earlier, withdrawal symptoms will be at their peak during the first few days. This first week, I want you to concentrate on *strength*. This word needs to be uttered during your prayers. Each day this week, I will provide scripture that focuses on strength. Throughout the day, pray and meditate on that scripture, especially when temptation is overbearing. Along with scripture, I will also provide information on the positive changes going on inside your body or some other useful smoking fact. I purposely withheld much of this information in other parts of the book, because I felt it would provide further encouragement on your daily journey in quitting.

Day 1.

The Sovereign LORD is my strength;
he makes my feet like the feet of a deer,
he enables me to go on the heights. (Habakkuk 3:19, NIV)

Tidbit:

Within...

20 minutes (of quitting): your blood pressure, pulse rate, and the temperature of your hands and feet will all return to normal. **8 hours**: your blood oxygen level will have increased to normal and carbon monoxide levels will have dropped to normal.

Within…

24 hours: your risk of a heart attack will have decreased by 50%.

1990 U.S. Surgeon General's Report on the "Health Benefits of Smoking Cessation," U.S. National Institute of Health, Medline Plus.

Day 2.

The LORD is for me, so I will have no fear.
What can mere people do to me?
Yes, the LORD is for me; he will help me.
I will look in triumph at those who hate me. (Psalms 118:6-
7 NLT)

Tidbit:

Within…

48 hours: Damaged nerve endings have started to re-grow and your sense of smell and taste are beginning to return to normal.

1990 U.S. Surgeon General's Report on the "Health Benefits of Smoking Cessation," U.S. National Institute of Health, Medline Plus.

Day 3.

As soon as I pray, you answer me; you encourage me by giving me strength. (Psalms 138:3 NLT)

Tidbit:

Within…

72 hours: Your entire body will test 100% nicotine-free and over 90% of all nicotine metabolites will now have passed from your body via your urine. You can also expect the symptoms of chemical withdrawal to have peaked in intensity. Your bronchial tubes are beginning to relax, thus making it easier to breathe. Your lung capacity has also started to increase.

1990 U.S. Surgeon General's Report on the "Health Benefits of Smoking Cessation," U.S. National Institute of Health, Medline Plus.

Day 4.

The LORD is my strength and my shield;
my heart trusts in him, and I am helped.
My heart leaps for joy and I will give thanks to him in song.
(Psalms 28:7 NIV)

Tidbit:

There appears to be a correlation between a country's standard of living, level of education and income, and the number of people who have quit smoking. *The more and better-informed people are, the more likely they are to quit smoking.*

(www.ezinearticles.com – 21 shocking smoking facts)

Day 5.

My flesh and my heart may fail, but God is the Rock and firm Strength of my heart and my Portion forever. (Psalms 73:26 Amplified Bible)

Tidbit:

The CDC found that smoking continues to be the leading cause of preventable death in the U.S., resulting in an estimated 440,000 premature deaths annually from 1995 through 1999. On average, adult men and women *smokers lost 13.2 and 14.5 years of life*, respectively, because they smoked.

(www.cancer.org – smoking costs)

Day 6.

Be of good courage,
And He shall strengthen your heart,
All you who hope in the LORD. (Psalms 31:24 NKJV)

Tidbit:

In the U.S., smoking kills more people than cocaine, heroin, alcohol, fire, automobile accidents, homicides, suicides, and AIDS combined.

(www.costkids.org – tobacco)

Day 7.

But as for you, be strong and do not give up, for your work will be rewarded.

(2 Chron. 15:7 NIV)

Tidbit:

Before taxes, the average cost of cigarettes in the U.S. is $3.81/pack. (www.tobaccofreekids.org)

This past week you saved: (not including taxes)

1 pack/day—You saved $26.67 this past week.

2 packs/day—You saved $53.34 this past week.

3 packs/day—You saved $80.01 this past week.

Congratulations on getting past this first week. You have likely gotten through the most difficult part of your journey

WEEK 2

Getting through week one was a great accomplishment. The big hurdle this past week was overcoming many of the physical symptoms associated with quitting. If you were using a nicotine substitute, this may have helped with some of that. This next week the focus is going to be temptation. Remember, I truly believe you do not have to be addicted to something to be tempted to do it. That being said, you are going to be bombarded with thoughts and doubts about whether you can continue on this journey. God's word provides plenty of hope on this very issue.

Day 8

No temptation has seized you except what is common to man. And God is faithful; he will not let you be tempted beyond what you can bear. But when you are tempted, he will also provide a way out so that you can stand up under it. (1 Cor. 10:13 NIV)

Tidbit:

If you have ever doubted that smoking affects your physical appearance, people that smoke have 10 times as many wrinkles as a person that does not smoke.

(www.alltrivia.net – facts about smoking)

Day 9

Keep awake and watch and pray [constantly], that you may not enter into temptation; the spirit indeed is willing, but the flesh is weak. (Mark 14:38 Amplified Bible)

Tidbit:

Every eight seconds someone dies from tobacco use...that's about as long as it takes to read this sentence.

(www.thestopsmokingguide.com – smoking facts)

Day 10

God blesses those who patiently endure testing and temptation. Afterward they will receive the crown of life that God has promised to those who love him. (James 1:12 NLT)

Tidbit:

I like to invest money. This came from MSN money on June 5, 2007.

The costs add up: Cigarettes, dry cleaning, and insurance -- you can even lose your job. A 40-year-old who quits and puts the savings into a 401(k) could save almost $250,000 by age 70.

(http://articles.moneycentral.msn.com/Insurance/InsureYou rHealth/HighCostOfSmoking.aspx?page=2)

Day 11

And do not lead us into temptation, but deliver us from the evil one. For Yours is the kingdom and the power and the glory forever. Amen. (Matt. 6:13 NIV)

Tidbit:

Secondhand smoke causes approximately 3,400 lung cancer deaths and 46,000 heart disease deaths in adult nonsmokers in the United States each year.

California Environmental Protection Agency. Identification of Environmental Tobacco Smoke as a Toxic Air Contaminant. Executive Summary. June 2005.

Day 12

For we do not have a High Priest who is unable to understand and sympathize and have a shared feeling with our weaknesses and infirmities and liability to the assaults of temptation, but One Who has been tempted in every respect as we are, yet without sinning. (Heb. 4:15 Amplified Bible)

Tidbit:

Secondhand smoke is classified by the EPA as a known human carcinogen (cancer causing).

(www.alltrivia.net – facts about smoking)

Day 13

...the Lord knoweth how to deliver the godly out of temptation....

(2 Peter 2:9 KJV)

Tidbit:

10 days to 2 weeks*: your brain and body have now physically adjusted to again functioning without nicotine, and the more than 3,500 chemical particles and 500 gases present in each and every puff.*

1990 U.S. Surgeon General's Report on the "Health Benefits of Smoking Cessation," U.S. National Institute of Health, Medline Plus.

Day 14

Blessed are those whose way is blameless, who walk in the law of the Lord. Blessed are those who keep his testimonies, who seek him with their whole heart.

(Psalms 119: 1-2 RSV)

Tidbit:

You have now completed the second week of your journey. Here is your total savings on cigarettes purchases alone.

You saved: (not including taxes)

1 pack/day—You saved $52.54 these past 2 weeks.

2 packs/day—You saved $106.68 these past 2 weeks.

3 packs/day—You saved $160.02 these past 2 weeks.

Congratulations on getting past the second week. You have faced and defeated a lot of obstacles!!!

WEEK 3

Overcoming the first two weeks and the hurdles associated with them may open the door for a letdown. Oftentimes in life when we face and overcome huge obstacles, it isn't uncommon to let our guard down. This week, I want to focus on perseverance. We will continue to look at some interesting facts and "tidbits" focusing on the "psychology" of smoking.

Day 15

The Lord himself goes before you and will be with you; he will never leave you nor forsake you. Do not be afraid; do not be discouraged. (Deut. 31:8 NIV)

Tidbit:

Your appeal to the opposite sex could triple as a non-smoker.

Psychological Reports. V3(2):1299-1306.

Day 16

*For you have need of endurance, so that when you have
done the will of God, you may receive what was promised.
(Hebrews 10:36 NASB)*

Tidbit:

Even smokers view non-smokers more positively than they
do smokers.

Journal of Applied Social Psychology. 16(8):702-725.

Day 17

I have fought a good fight, I have finished my course, I have kept the faith.

(2 Timothy 4:7 KJV)

Tidbit:

As a non-smoker, others may perceive you as being more self-disciplined than as a smoker.

British Journal of Addiction. 84(8):935-941.

Day 18

*Those who hope in the LORD will renew their strength.
They will soar on wings like eagles; they will run and not
grow weary, they will walk and not be faint.*

(Isa. 40:31 NIV)

Tidbit:

Non-smokers are viewed as more desirable to date than
smokers.

Psychological Reports. 83(3, Pt 2):1299-1306.

Day 19

The LORD's unfailing love surrounds the man who trusts in him.

(Psalms 32:10 NIV)

Tidbit:

Did you know that by avoiding typical "cues" to smoke that the likelihood of remaining smoke-free is doubled?

Velicer, WF; Prochaska, JO. 1999. An expert system intervention for smoking cessation. Patient Education & Counseling. V36(2):119-129.

Day 20

I can do everything through him that gives me strength.

(Phil. 4:13 NIV)

Tidbit:

Using cessation materials directly increases your chances of quitting smoking.

This would include this book, devotional and prayers.

Journal of Consulting and Clinical Psychology. 61(5):790-803

Day 21

And whatsoever ye do, do it heartily.
(Colossians 3:23 KJV)

Tidbit:

You saved (not including taxes)

1 pack/day—You saved $78.81 these past 3 weeks.

2 packs/day—You saved $160.02 these past 3 weeks.

3 packs/day—You saved $240.03 these past 3 weeks.

Congratulations on getting past the third week. You have gotten past this "hump" week and have really increased your chances of quitting.

WEEK 4

In week four we are going to really focus on grace. You are now on the fast track to recovery over your addiction. It can become easy to be consumed by pride and look down upon those with similar vices. I will provide verses that talk about grace and pride. We need to look at others as Jesus looks at us. I will also discuss the health benefits of quitting smoking that go beyond this month and into the rest of your life.

Day 22

...for all have sinned and fall short of the glory of God, and are justified freely by his grace through the redemption that came by Christ Jesus.

(Rom. 3:23,24 NIV)

Tidbit:

3 weeks to 3 months: your circulation has substantially improved. Walking has become easier. Your chronic cough, if any, has likely disappeared. Your overall lung function has improved up to thirty percent.

1990 U.S. Surgeon General's Report on the "Health Benefits of Smoking Cessation," U.S. National Institute of Health, Medline Plus.

Day 23

A man's pride shall bring him low: but honor shall uphold the humble in spirit.

(Prov. 29:23 KJV)

Tidbit:

1 to 9 months: any sinus congestion, fatigue, and shortness of breath have decreased. Cilia have reground in your lungs, thereby increasing their ability to handle mucus, keep your lungs clean, and reduce infections. Your body's overall energy has increased.

1990 U.S. Surgeon General's Report on the "Health Benefits of Smoking Cessation," U.S. National Institute of Health, Medline Plus.

Day 24

For it is by grace you have been saved, through faith—and
this not from yourselves, it is the gift of God—not by works,
so that no one can boast.

(Eph. 2:8-9 NIV)

Tidbit:

1 year*:* Your excess risk of coronary heart disease has
dropped to less than half that of a smoker.

1990 U.S. Surgeon General's Report on the "Health
Benefits of Smoking Cessation," U.S. National Institute of
Health, Medline Plus.

Day 25

Do nothing from selfishness or empty conceit, but with humility of mind regard one another as more important than yourselves.

(Phil. 2:3 NASB)

Tidbit:

5 to 15 years: your risk of stroke has declined to that of a non-smoker.

1990 U.S. Surgeon General's Report on the "Health Benefits of Smoking Cessation," U.S. National Institute of Health, Medline Plus

Day 26

You therefore, my son, be strong in the grace that is in Christ Jesus.

(2 Tim. 2:1 NKJV)

Tidbit:

10 years: *your risk of death from lung cancer has declined by almost half if you were an average smoker (one pack per day). Your risk of cancer of the mouth, throat and esophagus is now half that of a smoker's.*

1990 U.S. Surgeon General's Report on the "Health Benefits of Smoking Cessation," U.S. National Institute of Health, Medline Plus.

Day 27

...and all of you, clothe yourselves with humility toward one another, for God is opposed to the proud, but gives grace to the humble.

(1 Peter 5:5 NASB)

Tidbit:

15 years: your risk of coronary heart disease is now that of a person who has never smoked. Risk of lung cancer has decreased by 80 to 90%. Your overall risk of death has returned to near that of a person who has never smoked.

1990 U.S. Surgeon General's Report on the "Health Benefits of Smoking Cessation," U.S. National Institute of Health, Medline Plus.

Day 28

Let us then approach the throne of grace with confidence, so that we may receive mercy and find grace to help us in our time of need.

(Heb. 4:16 NIV)

Tidbit:

I think you are getting the picture with my money savings calculator. What I did want to do is extend it out to one year. Check out the financial impact that quitting smoking can have on your life.

These figures do not include taxes!

1 pack/day—You will save $1,386.84 this next year!

2 packs/day—You will save $2,773.68 this next year!

3 packs/day—You will save $4,160.52 this next year!

You've made it through the 28-day devotional. This by no means guarantees your long-term success in quitting. What it does do is lay a strong foundation in your physical and spiritual resolve. Anything without a sound foundation is not going to withstand the storms down the road.

*"The rain came down, the streams rose, and the winds blew and beat against that house; yet it did not fall, **because it had its foundation on the rock"** (Matt. 7:25).*

You need to continue to use God's word, His sword, on a daily basis. You also need to reflect on the positives that came from your quitting. And most importantly, you need to give God all the glory. May He continue to bless you in your life's journey.

GLOSSARY

Alveoli- Microscopic (300 million) air sacs in the lungs where oxygen and carbon dioxide exchange.

Aerosol- A way to administer inhaled medications.

Bleb- (See Bulla) This is an air pocket in the lung as a result of emphysema. This pocket can "pop" and cause the lung to collapse. Can also be called a bulla.

Bulla- (See Bleb) This is an air pocket resulting from emphysema. This pocket can "pop" as well and cause the lung to collapse. Can also be called a bleb.

Bronchial Tree- Term that describes the bronchial tubes which start out larger and get smaller as they work their way into the lungs.

Cancer- Formation of abnormal or mutated cells that grow into obstruction tumors.

Cilia- Microscopic hairs that "sweep" dirt, dust, and mucus out of the lungs, helping keep them clean.

CO2 (Carbon Dioxide)- Colorless, odorless gas that is produced in the body when cells break down. CO2 is exchanged with oxygen in the alveoli and is exhaled during breathing.

CVD (Cardiovascular Vascular Disease)- Disease that affects the arteries in the heart, which in turn can kill the muscle of the heart and affect its ability to pump blood.

Diaphragm- Dome-shaped muscle that sits at the base of each lung. The muscles contract or flatten, drawing air into the lungs.

Habit- Doing the same thing the same way all the time so that it becomes routine.

Metered Dose Inhaler (MDI)- Another way to take inhaled medications. It is also called a "puffer".

Mucus- Substance produced inside the lungs that aids in the clearance of foreign materials in the lungs.

Nerve- A fiber bundle that conducts electrical impulses from the brain and spine to the rest of the body. They control the body's organs.

Nicotine- The addictive chemical found in cigarettes.

O2 (Oxygen)- Gas that is breathed and essential for humans to survive.

PVD (Peripheral Vascular Disease)- A disease that affects the small arteries in the extremities of the body, such as hands and feet.

Rales- Breath sound heard by a stethoscope as a result of fluid in small airways and alveoli.

Rhonchi- Breath sound heard by a stethoscope as a result of secretions in the larger airways.

Secondhand Smoke- Also called environmental tobacco smoke (ETS). This is the smoke exhaled from pipes, cigars, or cigarettes along with the smoke exhaled by the smoker.

Sinus- An air sac or cavity in the cranium.

System- In medical terms, this term applies the designation of different bodily functions. (i.e. Renal, Pulmonary and Cardiac)

Tobacco- Substance found cigarettes, pipes, cigars, snuff and chewing tobacco.

Tumor- Abnormal growth of cells that can be cancerous or benign.

Trachea- Also called the "windpipe". This is the main airway that divides into the left and right mainstem airways, which then leads to the left and right lungs.

Wheeze- Breath sound resulting from constricted or inflamed airways. Wheezing is often described as a whistling sound.

CPSIA information can be obtained
at www.ICGtesting.com
Printed in the USA
LVHW020729261218
601737LV00001B/133/P